HISTORY ENCYCLOPEDIA

WORLD WAR II AND INDIA'S FREEDOM STRUGGLE

Contents

The Japanese Surrender	3
End of Japanese War	5
End of European Colonialism	6
Europe after World War II	7
Far East after World War II	8
The British Rule	10
Mutiny of 1857	12
End of the East India Company	13
Formation of Indian National Congress	14
Massacre at Jallianwala Bagh	16
Non-cooperation Movement	18
Civil Disobedience Movement	20
Dandi March	22
Rise of Gandhi	23
Rise of the Muslim League	24
Second Round Table Conference	25
Impact of World War II on Indian Freedom Struggle	26
Quit India Movement	28
Partition of India	30
India Granted Independence	31
Freedom at Midnight	32

WORLD WAR II AND INDIA'S FREEDOM STRUGGLE

The Japanese Surrender

1945

By the summer of 1945, the Japanese navy and air force had been decimated. Further, the Allies had blocked access to the seas and were conducting bomb raids over Japan, leaving the country in shambles. With the US capture of Okinawa, it was inevitable that the Allies would invade the main Japanese islands. US General Douglas MacArthur was to launch Operation Downfall in November 1945, but it was abandoned as Japan agreed to surrender.

Charred bodies lie amidst the destruction caused by the atomic bombing of Nagasaki.

Potsdam Declaration

The Allies issued the Potsdam Declaration that demanded unconditional surrender of the Japanese armed forces and if they did not accept the declaration then they would be responsible for the devastation that was to follow the country.

Japanese Prime Minister Kantaro Suzuki told the press that his government would not heed the ultimatum of the Allied powers.

After this, US President Harry Truman gave the order for the devastation to begin, which started with the dropping of the atomic bomb on Hiroshima by the US B-29 bomber Enola Gay.

On 8th August, 1945 USSR declared war against Japan, and a few days later the Soviet forces attacked Manchuria. This was quickly followed by the dropping of a second atomic bomb on the Japanese coastal city of Nagasaki, killing 39,000-80,000 people. Over the following months, many more died due to exposure to radiation.

Douglas MacArthur

Effects of the bombing

The atomic bombing of Hiroshima killed around 80,000 people and fatally wounded many more. Even after the Hiroshima attack, members from Japan's Supreme War Council were in favour of surrender, but the majority remained steadfast in their resistance to unconditional surrender.

FAST FACT

The Japanese were guilty of many war crimes during World War II and were responsible for the death of more than 20 million Chinese under a terrible policy called "Kill All, Burn All and Loot All".

Battleship Missouri Memorial at Pearl Harbor in Honolulu on the island of O'ahu. Japan surrendered aboard the deck to end World War II.

HISTORY ENCYCLOPEDIA

A costly battle

After the atomic attacks, the US planned to invade Japan under Operation Downfall in November 1945. However, the August atomic bombing of Hiroshima and Nagasaki and the Soviet invasion of Manchuria brought Japan to its knees. Faced with further destruction, Emperor Hirohito decided to surrender.

In response, the USA sent a message on 12th August, 1945 that "the authority of the Japanese emperor and government would be subject to the Supreme Commander of the Allied Powers". After a debate, Emperor Hirohito got work started on the wording of Japan's official surrender.

US 21st Bomber Command dropped incendiary bombs on Osaka, Japan on 1st June, 1945.

Military coup crushed

On 15th August, 1945, Major Kenji Hatanaka took over control of the imperial palace and the military coup managed to burn down Prime Minister Suzuki's residence.

However, the coup was soon squashed. By noon, Emperor Hirohito made a national address on the radio telling people that the country was about to surrender to the Allies.

Japan surrenders

USA accepted Japan's surrender. MacArthur led the Allied occupation of Japan as the Supreme Commander of the Allied Powers.

On 2nd September, 1945, Japan surrendered on the battleship, the USS *Missouri* in Tokyo Bay, Japan. The final surrender ceremony was stalled till the rest of the Allied delegates arrived.

In front of the Allied representatives, Japanese Foreign Minister Mamoru Shigemitsu and General Yoshijiro Umezu signed the Japanese Instrument of Surrender.

End of World War II

MacArthur signed on behalf of Allied forces, who made a declaration that "a better world shall emerge out of the blood and carnage of the past".

USS *Missouri* Battleship at Pearl Harbor in Hawaii.

Soon, the other allies including China, Britain, the USSR, Australia, Canada, France, the Netherlands and New Zealand signed the agreement and finally World War II came to an end. However, the war formally came to an end when the Treaty of San Francisco was enforced on 28th April, 1952.

1945: Atomic bombing of Japan
1945: Japan surrenders and World War II ends

Huge crowd packed in Times Square, in a premature celebration of Japan's surrender.

WORLD WAR II AND INDIA'S FREEDOM STRUGGLE

End of Japanese War

The US forces were making strides towards Japan and were increasingly relying on air warfare. Aerial bombing was the focal point of the US strategy for Japan. This strategy began with the dropping of 2000 tons of incendiary bombs over the city of Tokyo. Conducted over two days, the bombing completely burned more than 16 sq km of land in and around Tokyo—the Japanese capital.

Tokyo burns under B-29 firebomb assault. In this raid, 464 B-29s fire bombed the area immediately south of the Imperial Palace on 26th May, 1945.

Bombing of Tokyo

The Tokyo bombings were crucial for USA in terms of the devastation that it caused in the Japanese capital. It killed around 80,000-130,000 Japanese in a single fire-storm, making it the worst of its kind in history. From 1944 to 1945, the US forces carried on with the continuous long-range bombing of Japan using B-29 bombers. But the US forces had other plans for the island of Iwo Jima, because they realised that if Iwo Jima was captured, then it would become an important base for USA.

Raising the flag on Mount Suribachi

Joe Rosenthal took the historic photograph of *Raising the Flag on Iwo Jima* on 23rd February, 1945. It shows five Marines and a US Navy corpsman hoisting a replacement American flag on top of Mount Suribachi. Later, Felix de Weldon used the picture to sculpt the 1954 Marine Corps War Memorial, next to Arlington National Cemetery.

Marine Corps War Memorial. The memorial features the statues of servicemen who raised the second US flag on Iwo Jima during World War II.

Tokyo's shanty town, where post-World War II homeless Japanese set up housekeeping in small huts during wartime bombing.

Iwo Jima attack

Iwo Jima was severely bombarded by the US troops using naval guns, rockets and napalm bombs, but the Japanese troops had protected the island very well and it seemed unaffected. The US marines and Japanese troops began fighting on 19th February. After fierce fighting, the US flag was planted on Mount Suribachi and the island was secured on 16th March, 1945. The attack saw Japanese casualties of over 21,000 and US casualties of over 6000.

1944-45: Aerial bombing of Tokyo
1945: Battle of Iwo Jima

HISTORY ENCYCLOPEDIA

End of European Colonialism

Soviet communistic background.

After 100 years of the Emancipation Proclamation, the African Americans in USA, especially in the southern states, were still living a segregated life with no right to vote and discrimination. Segregation remained a daily reality they had to face along with instances of violence owing to their skin colour. They had no access to public schools and bathrooms.

End of colonialism

World War II brought an end to European colonialism. Colonies were waking up to the concept of people power and many colonies both in Africa and Asia were revolting against their imperial rulers. Uprisings to seek independence and communism were also the effects of World War II. Countries in eastern Europe and China seemed influenced by Soviet Russia and soon became communist states.

Civil rights movement in USA

In USA, African Americans joined the civil rights movement under Dr Martin Luther King Jr, which aimed at ending racial discrimination and segregation of African Americans. Mahatma Gandhi's non-violence message was propagated during the civil rights movements in USA.

In South Africa, however, racial discrimination continued even under the new government

The Martin Luther King Jr Memorial located on National Mall on the Tidal Basin in Washington DC.

and apartheid or separateness in South Africa existed until 1994. Soon, a women's rights movement would also begin in USA.

Advances in technology

A space race began between the USA and USSR as each country tried to develop space programmes. Quickly, technology developed during the war became better and sophisticated, ranging from sonar, radar to the use of chemicals, plastics, etc.

FAST FACT
USA sent the first men on the moon on 20th July, 1969.

Bronze statue of Nelson Mandela in Johannesburg. Nelson Mandela is credited with peacefully ending apartheid in South Africa.

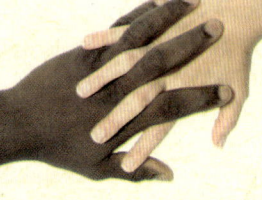

6

WORLD WAR II AND INDIA'S FREEDOM STRUGGLE

Europe after World War II

World War II had destroyed Europe, right from roads and bridges to communication. In all practical terms, Europe had to be rebuilt from scratch, but it was difficult since many governments did not have the resources to do so, since lot of money had been used during the war.

Europe overcomes the economic crisis

Countries like the USA were worried about the spread of communism and this meant that western Europe needed to be rebuilt quickly. The US economy and territory had not been greatly impacted because the war had not been fought on US soil. This made it the richest country in the world at the end of the war. Hence, the onus of helping Europe get over the economic crisis fell on the shoulders of USA.

The Marshall Plan

To help Europe pull through the after effects of the war, the US came up with the Marshall Plan, named after US Secretary of State George Marshall. It envisaged providing assistance and financial help to European countries to help them recover from the impact of World War II. Also known as the European Recovery Program, the Plan managed to channel over $13 billion to support the European economic recovery in the years after the World War II, especially between 1948 and 1951. The Plan managed to revive the economy and restore confidence of the people of Europe.

Assistance by the USA

By 1948, the USA had given $13 billion as assistance to west European countries and also to Soviet Russia, which did not accept the financial help. Although Japan was not part of the Marshall Plan, USA also offered financial assistance to the Asian country. At the end of the funding, the economies of most of the European countries were able to make a recovery.

George Marshall, US Secretary of Sate.

FAST FACT

George Marshall was awarded the 1953 Nobel Peace Prize for his Marshall Plan.

HISTORY ENCYCLOPEDIA

Far East after World War II

The destruction left in the wake of World War II in China made a country that was already suffering from overpopulation, underdevelopment and over 50 years of war and political unrest, even more wretched. Japanese forces had taken over quite a bit of the Chinese territory and it did not help that the Chinese economy was in depression. After indiscriminate bombing fighting, famines and epidemics, cities and villages were left in shambles.

China Carries On poster by United China Relief, member agency of the National War Fund.

State of Japan

Japan saw 14 million civilian deaths during World War II. The Japanese had a forced labour system where many civilians and prisoners of war who eventually died in these camps. It is also said that the Japanese also massacred many civilians eerily similar to that of the Nazis.

Indian fate

India suffered a similar fate. Famines were a part of life and the Indians could not pay the heavy taxes levied by the colonial rulers. Philippines had also suffered under its three years of occupation by Japan. Owing to World War II, the British altered its stand towards India because Britain required India's labour and manpower to help them fight the war. It was agreed upon that in exchange for India's support during World War II, it would offer Indians more political power.

Japan in ruins

Japan was in a bad shape due to the arbitrary aerial bombing and dropping of the atomic bomb. Almost 40 per cent of Japanese cities were destroyed and thousands rendered homeless.

The aftereffects of the atomic bombings included the debilitating effect of radiation, which continued to have repercussions several years after the atomic bombings.

FAST FACT

Japan and the Soviet Union made peace when they signed the Soviet–Japanese Joint Declaration of 1956.

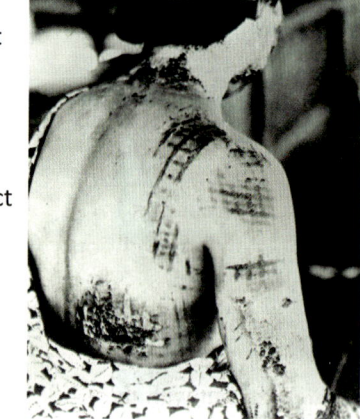

Injured female survivor of the Nagasaki atomic bombing. Her skin is burned in a pattern corresponding to the dark portions of a kimono worn at the time of the explosion.

Mother of a starving child begging in India in 1943.

Three Chinese civilians in Chungking witness a Japanese air-raid.

Independence Struggle of the World's Largest Democracy

The history behind Indian independence is about India's struggle by millions of faceless Indians, who fought for the freedom of their country. The year 1857 is often referred to as a benchmark in the history of Indian independence, which later turned into a Sepoy Mutiny by Indian soldier Mangal Pandey. Pandey was hanged and this fanned the revolution further, but soon the revolt was eventually stopped by the British army.

The beginning of the 1900s saw several revolutionary groups emerge in different parts of the country including Bengal, Punjab, Gujarat, Assam and the southern states. Political groups like the Congress came together to voice out the suffering of million natives to the British Empire in a peaceful manner. The prominent leaders of this period were Mahatma Gandhi, Subhash Chandra Bose, Jawaharlal Nehru and Lala Lajpat Rai. The revolutionaries who took extreme measures to gain freedom included Surya Sen, Chandrasekhar Azad and Bhagat Singh.

Mahatma Gandhi's "Salt March" and the 1942's "Quit India Movement" saw public support swell for the freedom movement. The British Government imprisoned many leaders including Gandhi. Subhash Chandra Bose moved away from Congress and formed a new party named the All India Forward Block Party and started his own army called Indian National Army (INA) and tried to win freedom, but with the sudden death of Netaji the INA attempts became unsuccessful.

HISTORY ENCYCLOPEDIA

The British Rule

In 1858, British Crown rule was established in India; thus, ending more than 100 years of control under the East India Company, after the Indian Mutiny or the "First War of Indian Independence". This changed the structure of the political, social and economic rule that the British had established.

FAST FACT

E. M. Forster's, "A Passage to India" has good insights into the racial and social isolation towards native Indians, practiced by the British that continued right till the end of British Raj.

After effects of the Mutiny of 1857

The Indian Mutiny had an impact on the country despite its failure. First, it made the British sit up and take note of the activities of the East India Company and therefore abolished it. They successfully ended the Mughal Empire and soon Queen Victoria was announced as the ruler of India. This announcement automatically meant that Britain now had control over the previously controlled Indian territories by the East India Company.

Negotiating with the British

Even as the country was under the East India Company prior to the mutiny, it should be noted that nearly two-fifths of the sub-continent was independently governed by over 560 large and small principalities. A few had turned against the British in the mutiny, but soon entered into negotiations with the British Raj.

Old illustration of British soldiers battling insurgents near Delhi.

Then, these princely states would become allies of the British who would help England with both financial and military support during the two world wars. The Nizam of Hyderabad is a good example of this.

Rise of nationalism

The rise of nationalism had made Britain understand that they would now have to work towards some amount of development of the country. They focussed a little on education under which the Ilbert bill was made, which stated that Indians could be as qualified and experienced as any Briton. However, in its true implementation, very few British people accepted Indians as equals; the majority felt that they were superior and more civilised than Indians.

Queen Victoria was proclaimed the first ruler of India after the fall of the Mughal Empire.

WORLD WAR II AND INDIA'S FREEDOM STRUGGLE

Old British Residency in Lucknow, India. Old derelict building which subject of a siege in the Indian Mutiny of 1857.

Growing racial gulf between Indians and British rulers

The Mutiny of 1857 created a racial gap between the Indians and British. This continued up until the end of the British Raj. E M Forster and Rudyard Kipling reflected this amply in their works. The British Empire appointed viceroys who had little experience about India and its people. It was only in 1917 that Edwin Montagu actually visited India on a fact-finding mission. It was understood then that just about a few thousand civil servants could not rule over 350 million Indians without having some Indians in the system.

Rudyard Kipling

1857: Indian mutiny
1917: Edwin Montagu visits India

British's economic benefits from India

Britain's main objective of being in India was because it made for a great economic investment. India was a good market for goods and services. Moreover, it required an army that the local natives had to pay for.

Investment in India under British Rule

In terms of investments, the British during their raj invested in infrastructure and built the railways network. They also built canals and other irrigation works and established the English education system.

An ancient palace of the Nizams in Hyderabad, India.

The British built a strong railway network that is operational even today.

Rise of industrialisation

The latter half of the nineteenth century witnessed some amount of industrialisation with the first cotton textile mill that was set up in 1853 in Bombay by Cowasjee Nanabhoy. Soon, the first jute mill was established in 1855 in Bengal. A majority of the modern Indian industries were controlled by the British. However, overall the raj only made a formerly prosperous country into shambles, where people were made poorer owing to heavy taxations that were levied under the British Rule and resulted in famines. A drained Indian economy had to bear the burden of an expensive British bureaucracy and army.

FAST FACT

Edwin Montagu became secretary of state for India in 1917 and worked on the British policy towards "progressive realisation of responsible government" in India and recommended control of some aspects of provincial government passed to Indian ministers.

HISTORY ENCYCLOPEDIA

Mutiny of 1857

William Hodson presented the heads of the two princes Mirza Mughal and Mirza Khizr Sultan. A scene in The Indian Mutiny, 1857.

In May 1857, Bengal army soldiers shot British officers and marched towards Delhi, and this mutiny added fuel to the rebellion that had started in northern and central India. The Revolt of 1857 was preceded by a series of instability in different parts of the country from the late eighteenth century onwards.

Start of the mutiny

Often referred to as the "First War of Indian Independence", it started with a series of rebellions in northern and central India against the British power and soon became the first united rebellion against the British in 1857-1858. Mangal Pandey, a Sepoy in the colonial British army, spearheaded the revolt, when he questioned British officers over violation of their religious beliefs. The introduction of the new cartridge for the Enfield rifle provoked the soldiers because the cartridges were wrapped in paper, coated with animal grease, making them offensive to both Muslims and Hindus.

Growing support for the mutiny

The uprising grew into a bigger rebellion when Mughal Emperor, Bahadur Shah, supported it. Soon, the mutiny of soldiers transformed into a revolutionary war, with many Indian chiefs hastened to support it at the behest of Bahadur Shah, who wrote letters to all the heads and Indian rulers requesting them to come together to create a sort of a union of Indian states to counterattack the British regime. Soon, the Bengal army joined it followed by different parts of the country from Awadh, Rohilkhand, to Bundelkhand, then further towards central India and Bihar and East Punjab. Later, other princely support was received when other leaders like Rani Laxmibai of Jhansi and Tatya Tope joined in.

Statue of Rani Laxmibai of Jhansi.

A painting depicting the Mutiny of 1857.

Memorial to those who died in the siege of Lucknow during the Indian Mutiny of 1857.

WORLD WAR II AND INDIA'S FREEDOM STRUGGLE

End of the East India Company

From 1600 onwards, the East India Company, also known as the English East India Company, comprised the merchants of London, who traded into the East Indies, Southeast Asia and India. On 31st December, 1600 a group of merchants who called themselves as the East India Company were given monopoly privileges for trade with East India.

Sir William James Erasmus Wilson

Move to China

In 1608, Sir Thomas Roe sought support from Mughal Emperor Jahangir after becoming an emissary of King James I in 1615. Soon, the Company established a factory at Surat. From the early eighteenth century, the trading entity soon embroiled itself into the local politics and became a British representative of the Queen in India. During the nineteenth century, the East India Company in China expanded and intensified British influence there.

The spice trade

The East India Company primarily wanted to have a pie in the spice trade share, which was originally monopolised by countries like Spain and Portugal. England defeated the Spanish Aramada in 1588, and soon England gained the control over the spice trade.

East India Company's trade expansion

The East India Company's rivalry with the Dutch East Indies from the East Indies led to struggles between the two. The East India Company traded with cotton, silk goods, indigo, salt and other spices from India. It soon expanded its activities from Persia to India.

Its gradual decline

The monopoly of East India led to the joining of hands of the United Company of Merchants of England trading to the East Indies. The Regulating Act of 1773 and Pitt's India Act of 1784 established government control and steadily the company lost commercial and political control. Later, it just became a representative of the British government in India and after the Indian uprising of 1857 it was brought to an abrupt end.

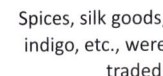

Spices, silk goods, indigo, etc., were traded.

The old silk route, which was used for trading silk between China and Sikkim, India.

13

HISTORY ENCYCLOPEDIA

Formation of Indian National Congress

Indian National Congress, by name Congress Party, was formed in 1885 and fought for India's independence from Britain. Lord Dufferin, the Viceroy of India, had implied that Indian intellectuals needed to have a forum to forward the grievances of Indians so that they could be better represented to the government.

Indian National Union

Mr Alan Octavian Hume, a retired member of Indian Civil Service, helped establish the organisation and named it Indian National union. The first session of the Indian National Union was held on 28th, 29th and 30th December, 1885, and was presided over by W C Banarjee, A O Hume, K T Telang, Subramanya Aiyar and Dadabhai Naroji. Dadabhai, known as the grand old man of India, suggested that the Indian National Union be re-named as Indian National Congress. It also envisioned on gathering opinions from educated Indians and attempting to make changes for the welfare of India.

Resolutions passed after the formation of Indian National Congress

The resolutions of the Congress included the abolition of the India Council to hold the Indian Civil Service Examination in India as well to increase the age limit for appearing in the Indian Civil Service Examination, to have elected members in legislative assemblies and to establish legislative assemblies in the North-West Frontier Province, Oudh and Punjab.

Aim of the Indian National Congress

The primary aim of the nascent national congress was to simply put in place a base towards the creation of a secular and democratic national movement, to make people politically aware, to put in place a headquarters for this and to ensure that it becomes an all-India leadership entity that could organically help create an anti-British strategy and anti-colonial mentality. Therefore, at the beginning the Congress started its functioning with very humble objectives.

THE FIRST INDIAN NATIONAL CONGRESS, 1885.

Image of the delegates to the first meeting of the Indian National Congress in Bombay, 1885.

A O Hume, Dadabhai Naroji and Wedderburn meeting at the Indian National Congress.

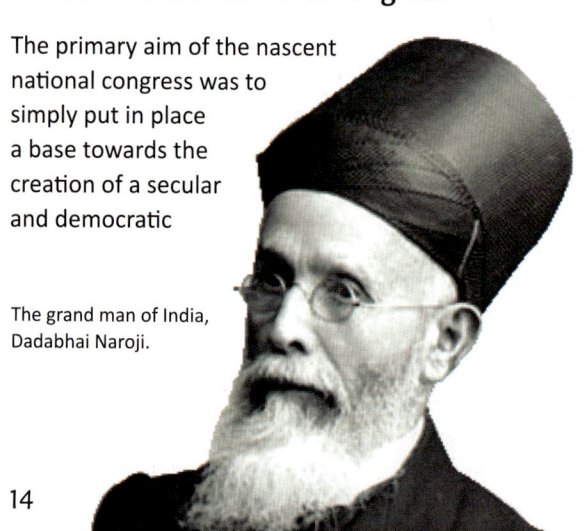

The grand man of India, Dadabhai Naroji.

FAST FACT

During the post Independence period, the last important episodes in the Congress involved the final step to independence and the division of the country on religious lines.

WORLD WAR II AND INDIA'S FREEDOM STRUGGLE

Mahatma Gandhi became a global symbol of peace due to his peaceful method of solving disputes of which one was the Boycott of British Goods.

FAST FACT

On 12th March, 1930, Mahatma Gandhi led the Dandi March to produce salt from seawater, which was considered illegal at the time due to the British monopoly over the salt market in India. This march led to various other non-violence movements.

Boycott of British goods

By the early twentieth century, the Congress began the "swadeshi" movement. This movement urged people to boycott all British goods and encouraged them to use goods that were produced indigenously.

British social reformer Annie Besant and Indian nationalist Bal Gangadhar Tilak started the Home Rule wing in 1917. This was known as the extremist wing of the Indian National Congress. It addressed the diverse social classes of the country and encouraged them to boycott British goods and practice passive resistance.

Between the 1920s and 1930s, the Congress endorsed nonviolent non-cooperation against the British rule under the leadership of Gandhi. The Indian National Congress led the nationwide civil disobedience movement and advocated for the revocation of the tax levied by the British.

Move towards self rule

Gandhi's Civil Disobedience Movement of 1930-31 was kickstarted by the Salt March and became a unique symbol of the civil resistance movement. It helped undermine British authority and in a way brought together different sections of India together towards a common cause under the Indian National Congress and also facilitated the next stage towards India's struggle towards self-rule.

Quit India Movement

At the start of World War II in 1939, Britain entered the war and unwittingly dragged India into it as well. This upset many in the Indian National Congress, who declared that they would not support the war effort until India attained total freedom from the British rule.

In order to bring the British rulers to the negotiating table, Gandhi initiated his "Quit India" movement in August 1942 with a call to "do or die". Intense non-violent resistance resulted in the imprisonment of most of the Congress leaders.

It was only after the war that the British government of Clement Attlee passed an independence bill (1947) and in January 1950, India's constitution as an independent state emerged.

1930: Civil Disobedience Movement
1950: India has a constitution

Discussing the "Quit India" movement with Nehru, 1942.

15

HISTORY ENCYCLOPEDIA

Massacre at Jallianwala Bagh

On 13th April, 1919 around 10,000 or more unarmed men, women and children gathered at the Amritsar's Jallianwala Bagh to attend a protest meeting, despite a ban on public meetings. General Dyer ordered his soldiers to fire into the gathering, and for 15 minutes 1,650 rounds of ammunition were unloaded into the screaming, terrified crowd, killing 400 civilians and wounding another 1200.

Before the massacre

In protest to the Rowlatt Act, Amritsar had observed a peace hartal on the 30th March and 6th April, 1919 and the British government wanted to repress the protest. On 10th April, 1919, Dr Satyapala and Dr Kitchlew, two popular leaders of the province, were deported from Amritsar.

Effect of the massacre

The massacre instigated and fuelled nationalist feelings across Indians and had a deep impact on the leaders of the freedom struggle particularly on Gandhi. Gandhi had promised Britain that India would support the colonial ruler in World War I. This was to help create a base toward granting partial autonomy for India, but post the Jallianwala Bagh massacre, Gandhi was of the opinion that India should stop this request for partial autonomy and seek, and fight for complete freedom and total independence. The Jallianwala Bagh massacre became the trigger for the next level of India's struggle towards freedom and propelled Gandhi to start off India's first civil resistance movement called as the civil disobedience movement against Britain's tyrannical rule.

The Jallianwala Bagh

Jallianwala Bagh was closed on all sides by houses and buildings and just a few narrow entrances, which were generally locked. The main entrance was a bit wide, but was secured by British troops. They had the backing of the armoured vehicles. There was no warning issued to disperse the crowds.

The main entrance was a bit wide, but was secured by British troops. They had the backing of the armoured vehicles. There was no warning issued.

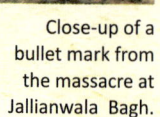

Close-up of a bullet mark from the massacre at Jallianwala Bagh.

Bullet-marked wall at Jallianwala Bagh, Amritsar, India.

FAST FACT

Although Queen Elizabeth II had not made any comments on the incident, during her state visits in 1961 and 1983, she spoke about the events at a state banquet in India on 13th October, 1997.

Jallianwala Bagh massacre

On Baisakhi day, Sunday 13th April, 1919, 50 British Indian Army soldiers, under orders from Brigadier-General Reginald Dyer were asked to reload their rifles many times and were ordered to shoot to kill.

Events of the massacre

"The Martyr's" well.

After the shooting, a number of people died in stampedes in their attempt to get away from the Bagh, but got caught at the narrow gates. A few jumped into the solitary well to escape the shooting. The wounded could not be shifted when the curfew was declared adding to the casualties.

Impact of the massacre

The Jallianwala tragedy had a deep impact. In fact, Rabindranath Tagore renounced his knighthood as a form of protest against the massacre. Gandhi returned the Kaisar-i-Hind medal given to him for his work during the Boer War. General Dyer's act was universally seen with contempt. Britain's prime minister too declared in the British parliament that the massacre was "one of the worst outrages in the whole of our history". However, Dyer found some support among senior British officers who appreciated his act and said that he was only trying to suppress another Indian Mutiny. The House of Commons debate censured his act and Winston Churchill stated, "The incident in Jallianwala Bagh was an extraordinary event, a monstrous event, an event which stands in singular and sinister isolation".

Jallianwala Bagh memorial in Amritsar, Punjab, India.

Hunter committee

The Jallianwala Bagh massacre brought forth strong public reaction in India and even in England. An enquiry committee was appointed to enquire about the massacre and Punjab disturbances. Indian National Congress boycotted the Hunter Committee and appointed another unofficial committee of popular lawyers, including Motilal Nehru, CR Das, Abbas Tyabji, MR Jayakar and Gandhi. Prior to the Hunter Committee beginning its proceeding, the government passed an Indemnity Act, which was criticised. General Dyer was found guilty of a "mistaken notion of duty" and was relieved of command.

1919: Jallianwala Bagh Massacre

1920: Dyer's commands are condemned

Monument of Rabindranath Tagore in Kolkata, India.

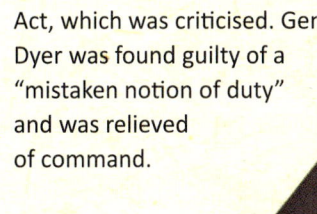
1600 rounds were fired by British troops from here on 20,000 innocent people.

HISTORY ENCYCLOPEDIA

Non-cooperation Movement

The non-cooperation movement was spearheaded under Gandhi from September 1920 to persuade the British government to give India its right to self-govern. The movement was fuelled by Amritsar's Jallianwala Bagh massacre, where the British had indiscriminately killed innocent and unarmed Indians. The movement also gathered more steam because Indians were unhappy at the government's inability at taking an action against General Dyer, the man responsible for the massacre.

What triggered this movement

Impoverished farmers in Champaran in Bihar and Kheda in Gujarat were pushed towards growing cash crops in place of food crops, such as tobacco, indigo and cotton instead of food crops. Famine also meant no respite from paying taxes. Indian revolutionaries like Sardar Vallabhbhai Patel, Jawaharlal Nehru and Rajendra Prasad came together with Mahatma Gandhi to work towards India's independence. Muslim leaders came together to form the Khilafat committee to fight the British. The Jallianwala Bagh massacre had angered everyone and soon Gandhi came up with the idea of nationwide Satyagraha against the Rowlatt Acts.

Proposing non-violence

Gandhi presented the proposal of non-cooperation in the Calcutta session of the Indian Nation Congress and stated that, "The English Government is Saitan. Cooperation is not possible with it". He added that the government was not sad at its actions so, "we have to adopt a progressive nonviolent non-cooperation policy for the fulfilment of our demands".

Gandhi's idea faces opposition

The non-cooperation movement was launched on 1st August, 1920 and after the Indian National Congress met for a special session at Calcutta on 4th September, 1920. Gandhiji's idea faced opposition from veteran leaders particularly C R Das who did not approve of the boycott of legislative council elections, because it was believed that boycotting the new Councils would alienate Indians further from the fountainhead of political power.

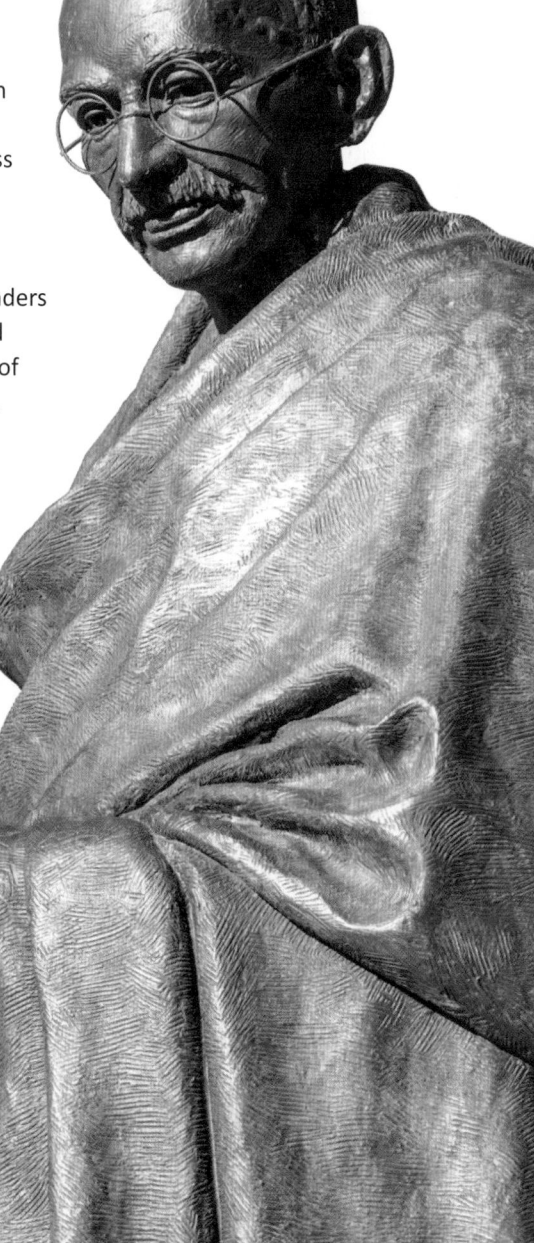

Statue of historic leader, Mahatma Gandhi, in Parliament Square, London.

Statue of Jawaharlal Nehru.

Monument of Sardar Vallabhbhai Patel (1875-1950).

WORLD WAR II AND INDIA'S FREEDOM STRUGGLE

Aim of the movement

The aim was simple: to non-violently look towards mobilising masses towards the creation of a nationalist feeling. India's first mass-based political movement under Gandhi boycotted the use of foreign cloth; the forthcoming visit of the Prince of Wales in November 1921 had popularised the use of the charkha and khadi, which lead to the Jail Bharo (fill the jail by arresting everyone) by Congress volunteers.

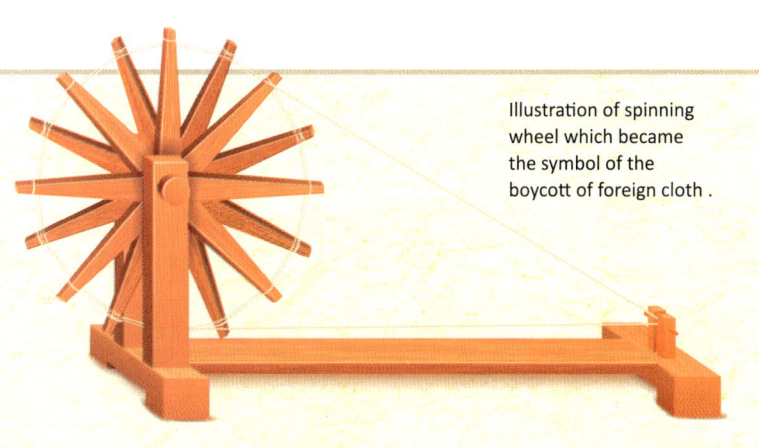

Illustration of spinning wheel which became the symbol of the boycott of foreign cloth.

Features of the movement

The non-cooperation movement or the "Asahayog Andolan" transformed the freedom struggle to another level since India's First War of Independence in 1857. It commenced in 1920 and its momentum lasted through 1922 with great support from the leaders and members of the Indian National Congress. The movement with its objective of resisting British rule via non-violence led to supporters of the movement refusing to purchase British goods and go back to using local handicrafts.

Elements of the movement

The largely non-violent movement urged people to resign titles, boycott government educational institutions, courts, government services, foreign goods, elections and also refuse to pay taxes.

Gandhi and Sardar Patel, Bardoli Satyagraha, 1928.

Violence erupts during the non-cooperation movement

In August 1921, the Muslim Moplah movement had violent altercations; this incident was followed by more violence in Chauri Chaura. Members of a Congress and Khilafat procession picketed the local bazaar in their bid to oppose liquor sales and high food prices. After being provoked by some policemen the crowd attacked them, in retaliation the police opened fire. And an enraged crowd killed 22 policemen and set the police station on fire. Gandhi called off the movement after this incident.

1920: INC meets for a special session

1921: Charkha and Khadi become popular

Gandhi during the Salt March, March 1930.

FAST FACT

Gandhi's commitment to non-violence was redeemed when (1930-1934) tens of millions again revolted in the Salt Satyagraha.

19

Civil Disobedience Movement

Gandhi during the freedom struggle in 1930.

Under Mahatma Gandhi's leadership, the Civil Disobedience Movement grew to become an important event in the history of India's freedom struggle. It started in 1930 and the main objective behind this movement was to challenge and confront the laws made by the British.

Gandhi's demands

Gandhi presented before Viceroy Lord Irwin a request that said that certain elements of the British Raj needs to be removed at an immediate basis and the list of demands given by him would need to be implemented else the civil resistance movement would be launched with the Dandi Satyagraha. The demands included the prohibition of intoxicants, change the ratio between the rupee and sterling, reduction of the land revenue rate, abolition of salt tax, reduction in military and civil administration expenditure among others.

Reasons behind the movement

The Simon Commission planned to appoint only British Parliament members to create a new constitution for India. The national political parties and social organisations across the nation rejected the commission. At Bombay's All-Party Conference of May 1928, formed to make more boycotts, gave Dr M A Ansari and Motilal Nehru the responsibility of the drafting committee to prepare the constitution for India. However, the British Government refused to pay heed to it. Soon, they were warned after the Calcutta Session of the INC in 1928 that it would start a Civil Disobedience Movement if India was not granted its own government.

Gandhi's demands

Mahatma Gandhi presented a request before Viceroy Lord Irwin, which said that certain elements of the British Raj needed to be removed at an immediate basis. He also stated that the list of demands given by him would need to be implemented, else the civil resistance movement would be launched with the Dandi Satyagraha. The demands included the prohibition of intoxicants, a change in the ratio between the rupee and sterling, reduction of the land revenue rate, abolition of salt tax, reduction in military and civil administration expenditure among others.

FAST FACT

Gandhi began the Salt March with a mere 78 followers, but this number grew to tens of thousands by the time he reached Dandi.

Mahatma Gandhi leading a movement.

WORLD WAR II AND INDIA'S FREEDOM STRUGGLE

India adopts civil disobedience

Mahatma Gandhi

The Civil Disobedience Movement began with the Dandi March, where Gandhi marched with his followers to protest against the taxes levied on salt. Millions joined his march and illegally picked up salt from the coastal areas.

This movement further gained momentum when people all over the country began boycotting British goods and services. Peasants began to risk their lands and livelihoods when they started refusing to pay taxes. Several forest laws imposed by the British government in Maharashtra, Karnataka and other central provinces were blatantly defied by the masses.

Calling-off the movement

The British were anxious on the increasing popularity of the movement and therefore arrested all major Congress leaders. In April 1930, Abdul Gaffar Khan, a political and spiritual leader and follower of Gandhi was arrested. His arrest led to protests, which were suppressed by the British who arrested around 10,000 protestors including women and children, and thrashed them. This made Gandhi call off the civil disobedience movement.

Gandhi–Irwin Pact

In March 1930, Gandhi signed the Gandhi-Irwin Pact with the Viceroy Lord Irwin that outlined two important elements; first, the participation of Congress in the round table conference and the calling off the civil disobedience movement. It was attended by Sarojini Naidu and Gandhi. The conference was held in London, but Lord Willingdon in Gandhi's absence adopted the repression policy violating the Gandhi-Irwin Pact. Soon, the civil disobedience movement started again.

Lord Irwin

Ordinances from the British Government

The Congress Working Committee came up with the decision to restart the civil disobedience movement by January 1932. To retaliate, the British Government came up with four ordinances to deal with the prevailing situation, wherein police could arrest anyone based on mere suspicion. Sardar Patel and Gandhi were arrested along with the supporters of Congress. The movement continued for six months. Gandhi fasted for 21 days from 8th May, 1933 and the movement finally came to an end on 7th April, 1934.

Salt march statue.

HISTORY ENCYCLOPEDIA

Dandi March

The Dandi March or Salt Satyagraha spearheaded by Gandhi started in March–April 1930 and became the first act of civil disobedience or satyagraha, where Gandhi garnered widespread support from Indians and soon became very popular for his staunch support to a non-violent movement.

Gandhi at Dandi, South Gujarat, picking salt on the beach at the end of the Salt March, 5th April, 1930. Behind him is his second son Manilal Gandhi and Mithuben Petit.

Protests against the salt tax

The production and distribution of salt within India had been under the control of the British, who had banned Indians from producing or selling it independently, which meant that Indians had to buy salt that was very expensive, because this commodity was heavily taxed. A great majority of poor Indians could not afford it and soon there was a public outcry over this, and protests against the salt tax began.

The Dandi March

At the start of 1930, Gandhi started a demonstration against the salt tax and marched into Gujarat from his Sabarmati Ashram to the town of Dandi near the Arabian Sea coast, accompanied by many followers. The march halted at different villages along the route, where more crowds would gather to listen to Gandhi who spoke against the unjust practice of taxing the poor. On 5th April, the group reached Dandi after a journey of 385 km and on 6th April, Gandhi and his followers picked up a handful of salt from the shore and proclaimed that they had broken the law.

Consequences of the march

Later, many were arrested and imprisoned, including Jawaharlal Nehru and Gandhi. The marches to other salt works continued with 2500 people under poetess Sarojini who were attacked and beaten by the police. At the end of these marches, around 60,000 freedom fighters were in jail. Gandhi after his release from jail started negotiations with Lord Irwin and a truce was declared. Soon, Gandhi, representing the Indian National Congress, was invited to attend the second session of the Round Table Conference in London.

A picture of Gandhi and Sarojini Naidu during the Dandi March.

WORLD WAR II AND INDIA'S FREEDOM STRUGGLE

Rise of Gandhi

Mohandas Karamchand Gandhi was born in Porbandar, to a wealthy family. He was the fourth child of Karamchand Gandhi and was an average student. At the age of 13, he was married to a girl named Kasturba. He studied law under his father's insistence, although he wanted to study medicine and went to England to pursue his education in 1888. After attaining bar in 1891, he tried to practice law in Rajkot and Bombay, with very little success.

"The weak can never forgive. Forgiveness is the attribute of the strong."
-Mahatma Gandhi

Quote by Mahatma Gandhi

Encounter with racism

Gandhi accepted an offer to represent a firm in Pretoria, the capital of Transvaal in the Union of South Africa. While travelling in a first-class train compartment in Natal, he was asked by a white man to leave the compartment. Gandhi got off the train and decided to work towards eliminating racism. He called for a meeting of Indians in Pretoria and spoke against the whites who practiced racial discrimination. This launched his campaign of improved legal status for Indians in South Africa, who suffered discrimination at that time. He was lynched by an angry mob when he aired his views against racism.

Gandhi returns to India

Gandhi returned to India in January 1915 and by then, he had attained the title of "Mahatma" for his simple life and the development of the concept of Satyagraha that he had started in South Africa. Gandhi spoke of a new, free India and convinced people to stand against the British rule. After the Jallianwala Bagh Massacre, he called for a non-cooperation movement against British institutions including British courts, stores and schools. He soon became an icon for the masses. He began the Khadi movement with the intention of making people spin their own clothing rather than buy British goods. His belief was that it would create employment and soon many could attain economic independence.

FAST FACT

Fasting was a protest technique that Gandhi believed in and he also was the one who started protest marches and his Dandi or salt march remains very popular incident in Indian History.

A waxwork of Mahatma Gandhi on display at Madame Tussauds.

23

HISTORY ENCYCLOPEDIA

Rise of the Muslim League

The Muslim League or the All India Muslim League was a political group that demanded for a separate Muslim state during the partition of British India in the year 1947. The Muslim League was a political organisation of India and Pakistan, and was founded in 1906 as the All-India Muslim League under Aga Khan III. The objective was simple to protect the political rights of Muslims in India. Founded in 1906 to preserve the rights of Indian Muslims, the Muslim League found favour with the British rulers. However, despite this show of encouragement from the British, the league called for a self-rule policy for India in 1913.

All India Muslim League.

Hindu–Muslim divide

Muhammad Ali Jinnah, the prominent leader from the Muslim league was a firm believer of Hindu–Muslim unity in a united and independent India. Only after 1940 that the league seemed to veer towards the formation of a separate Muslim state independent of British India. The fear within the league was that India in the present state would comprise many Hindus and India's Muslims would be a minority.

Decline of the Muslim league

Jinnah and the Muslim league spearheaded the struggle to partition British India into two different states, Hindu and Muslim. With the formation of Pakistan in 1947, the Muslim league became Pakistan's main political party and soon renamed the All Pakistan Muslim League. Gradually, the popularity of this league reduced in independent Pakistan and lost its power in East Pakistan or Bangladesh. A little later it again failed in West Pakistan and after numerous splits and factions in the 1960s the party disappeared by 1970.

Coin with the image of a portrait of Muhammad Ali Jinnah.

Indian leaders at the Simla Conference (1946). From left to right: Rajendra Prasad, Muhammad Ali Jinnah, C. Rajagopalachari, Maulana Abul Kalam Azad.

Gandhi and Jinnah in Bombay, September 1944.

FAST FACT

Jinnah forbade his doctor to disclose the fact that he was suffering from tuberculosis to the public. He was afraid that it would impact the freedom movement. However, Jinnah died of the same in 1948 and was buried in the heart of Karachi city.

WORLD WAR II AND INDIA'S FREEDOM STRUGGLE

Second Round Table Conference

The Simon Commission report did not provide adequate substance. The new Labour Government under Ramsay MacDonald in 1929 held a series of Round Table Conferences in London.

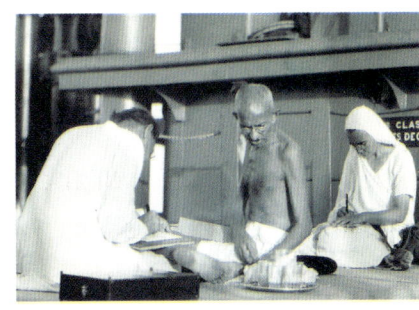

Gandhi and Mirabehn en route to London for the Round Table Conference, 1931.

First Round Table Conference

The first Round Table Conference convened in 1931 did not have much impact. It spoke of the development of India as a federation under which transfer of defence and finance would happen. But it seemed to be recommendations only on paper and civil disobedience continued unabated. The British Government soon understood that the Indian National Congress would need to be part of any decision pertaining to the formation of an Indian Government.

Gandhi meets Lord Irwin

During the civil disobedience movement, Viceroy Lord Irwin met Gandhi to arrive at a compromise. They arranged for Congress' participation in the Second Round Table Conference with the condition that the civil disobedience movement would be discontinued and that the government would withdraw all ordinances issued against the Congress. It was also decided that the government would withdraw all prosecutions relating to all non-violent offences and that they would release persons who were jailed for their involvement in the movement.

Second Round Table Conference

The Second Round Table Conference was held in London from 7th September to 1st December, 1931. Gandhi participated on behalf of the Indian National Congress. Just weeks prior to the proposed conference, the conservatives had come to power and it was felt that Gandhi could not be the sole representative of all Indian people. The Second Round Table Conference did not seem to get any major results for India and soon struggles against the British rule continued, and Gandhi was arrested along with other Congress leaders.

1929: New Labour Government
1931: Second Round Table Conference

During the Federal Structure Sub-committee meeting presided over by Lord Sankey, London, November 1931 (Round Table Conference).

HISTORY ENCYCLOPEDIA

Impact of World War II on Indian Freedom Struggle

In 1939, when the German troops invaded Poland, Britain and France declared war against Germany on 3rd September, 1939 and the start of World War II accelerated the end of British rule in India. During the war, leaders from the Indian National Congress stated that if British wanted India's cooperation, it must have the right of self-determination.

Limited Satyagraha

When the British refused to allow the right of self-determination for India, the provincial ministries under Congress resigned in 1939. By October 1940, they urged for a limited Satyagraha to ensure that it did not seriously hurt the war efforts. Many from Congress believed that a simple Satyagraha would not be enough to attain independence for India and aggression would be required.

Stafford Cripps Mission

In 1942, Britain faced pressure from USA and China to grant political power to India. With Burma's fall and rising pressure from Japan, Britain sent Sir Stafford Cripps to India in March 1942 to gain India's co-operation. The mission was also meant to convey to the local people that Britain would fulfil its past promise of a self-government by Indian people.

The mission also promised that post the war, immediate steps would be taken to put a body elected by the people in place to develop the constitution of India. However, the Stafford Cripps Mission assured dominion status with secession rights; immediate transfer of power was rejected. These assurances were rejected by the Indian leaders. Gandhi, as per the wishes of his Congress colleagues, called for a mass independent movement.

Sir Stafford Cripps

1939: Britain and France declare war against Germany

1942: Sir Stafford Cripps comes to India

Silhouette of troops at Pandu Ghat, India, enroute Myitkyina, Burma.

FAST FACT

Indian revolutionary Udham Singh, as a child, had seen his brother's killing at the Jallianwala Baugh massacre. He wanted to seek vengeance for his brother's death and after 21 years he killed Michael O'Dwyer, the governor of Punjab who had supported the massacre. Udham Singh was arrested and hanged in 1940.

WORLD WAR II AND INDIA'S FREEDOM STRUGGLE

Quit India Movement

British Governor-General of India, Lord Linlithgow, had dragged the Indian army into World War II without consulting Indian leaders. While the Muslim League supported the war, the Congress had divided opinions on the subject.

After the failure of the Cripps Mission, the Indian National Congress passed the Quit India resolution at the 1942 Bombay session. The focus was on the slogan "do or die", which was derived from Gandhi's speech that called for freeing India or dying in the attempt of doing so.

Gandhi launched the Quit India Movement in his bid to get Britain to negotiate and agree to India's call for freedom. He issued this call from the grounds of Bombay, where Indians were asked to "do or die" towards attaining freedom for India. The British government declared the movement illegal, and soon, the most important leaders were arrested.

Netaji Subhash Chandra Bose addressing a rally in Tokyo, 1945.

The INA was called the Azad Hind Fauj or "the Free India Army" and was re-organised with the creation of a second division. This time, it included a women's regiment, which was named the Rani Jhansi regiment.

INA losses and gains

The provisional government of free India declared war on Britain and captured large parts of Manipur. The Indian tricolour was raised on these captured lands. However, after the defeat of Japan and German forces, the INA had to retreat from Kohima. Many INA soldiers were arrested and died while fighting the British. Subhash Chandra Bose tried to escape to Japan, but he is said to have died in an air-crash on his way there.

Netaji Subhash Chandra Bose and Members of the Azad Hind Fauj.

Role of Indian National Army

Captain Mohan Singh came up with the idea of the INA and urged for Japan's help. Indian prisoners of war were given by the Japanese to Mohan Singh, who gathered and trained them to form the INA.

By 1942, the first division of the INA was formed with 16,300 men. However, shortly after the formation, differences between Mohan Singh and the Japanese erupted and the Captain was captured. Along with Rashbehari Bose, Subhash Chandra Bose went to Tokyo, where he received assurances that Japan had no territorial aspirations in India.

Netaji Subhash Chandra Bose

Quit India Movement

Launched under the leadership of Gandhi in 1942, the Quit India Movement protested against Britain for sending Indian troops to fight in World War II and insisted on the immediate independence of India. This movement was also called the August Movement and was launched by Gandhi in his bid towards attaining complete freedom for India. It was a movement and a call for mass non-violent protest, where Britain was to withdraw completely from India.

Policemen trying to control protestors.

Protestors of the Quit India Movement.

Support for the movement

Gandhi felt that the presence of the British in India was provoking Japan to attack them. This reason, combined with all the other problems that India was facing at the hands of the British, led Gandhi to passionately call upon his countrymen. He asked Indians who wanted freedom to "strive" for it and he urged every Indian to "do or die" in the attempt to attain India's freedom.

The Quit India Movement began soon after the talks between the Congress and British were unsuccessful. Many Indian leaders, including Gandhi, were put in jail for supporting this movement. There were protest demonstrations. These demonstrations had several violent manifestations, some of which resulted in bomb attacks and violence.

However, the Quit India Movement wasn't a popular choice and many opposed it. Straying away from the Congress stand, the Muslim League supported the British and opposed the Quit India movement. Many Indian businessmen did not support the movement because they believed that it would affect their business returns. In fact, even within the country, the movement lacked student support because the students were supporting Subhash Chandra Bose's struggle. Therefore, this movement didn't have the kind of support it needed to succeed.

Period of violence and revolts

Britain's response to the protests was to implement fines and usage of bombs against protestors. The movement, which had its base in non-violence, soon developed to include several violent protests. In 1946, the Indian Royal Navy struck work and, soon, the sailors too joined the movement. They were followed by the air force and local police forces. Riots and revolts began, and the "do or die" slogan became the mantra of the people of India.

FAST FACT

The Quit India Movement had three phases. The first phase involved processions and strikes. The second phase involved raiding government buildings. The third phase saw mobs retaliating against the police.

Policemen trying to hit demonstrators during the Quit India Movement in Bombay.

WORLD WAR II AND INDIA'S FREEDOM STRUGGLE

Arrest of prominent leaders

The country was facing unrest much before the Quit India movement began. Around this time, the British government decided to curb the retaliations by arresting several prominent and senior leaders of the Indian National Congress.

As the protests continued, the British authorities began to impose stricter rules. They soon declared that the Indian National Congress was an illegal formation. This led to more protests as people flocked the streets with more demonstrations and retaliations. Slogans like "Do or Die" were chanted during these processions and the movement was locally known as the "Bharat Chhodho Andolan".

Revered leaders like Maulana Abul Kalam Azad, Netaji Subhash Chandra Bose, Mahatma Gandhi, Muhammad Ali Jinnah, Asoka Mehta, Jaya Prakas Narayan, Jawaharlal Nehru, Sardar Vallabhbhai Patel, Dr Rajendra Prasad and Chakravarti Rajgopalachari were involved in the Quit India Movement. Many of them were jailed for their participation.

The place where Kasturba Gandhi rests in peace.

Gandhi gets arrested

After the Quit India resolution was passed at the Bombay session of the Indian National Congress, the British responded by imprisoning Gandhi. He was detained at the Aga Khan Palace in Pune. Other members of the Congress Party's National Leadership were arrested and imprisoned at the Ahmednagar Fort and the Congress party was banned. However, this only served to agitate the masses, who burned down government buildings, resorted to violence against the police and gathered in large masses to protest against the British.

Period of protests

The British authorities arrested over 100,000 Indians across the country and levied heavy fines. In some cases, the protestors were publicly flogged. Many innocent demonstrators were wounded and some even lost their lives in police and army fire. Some leaders went underground and continued the freedom struggle. They broadcasted messages over secret radio stations and distributed leaflets. British authorities wanted to take some senior Congress leaders like Gandhi out of the country to another country like Yemen or South Africa, but finally chose not to do so. While under arrest, Gandhi's wife, Kasturba Gandhi, and his personal secretary, Mahadev Desai, died.

It was easy for the British to curb the Quit India Movement due to its lack of co-ordination and clarity, but it also gave them a clear indication that their time as the ruler of India was nearing its end.

Gandhiji and Kasturba

FAST FACT

Mahatma Gandhi was nominated for the Nobel Peace Prize five times between 1937 and 1948. However, he never won the prize.

Partition of India

The struggle for independence against the British lasted for 90 long years. These years saw many rebellions, both small and large. The Indian National Congress spearheaded a major part of the freedom struggle, but the British authorities favoured the Muslim League. Eventually, the League demanded for a separate state and India was divided.

Reasons behind the partition

World War II fuelled a break in the relations between the British, Indian National Congress and Muslim League, because Britain expected India to be a part of the war and help by providing soldiers. However, the Congress opposed this as they saw no benefit for India to be part of the war. The Muslim League supported Britain because they wanted Britain's support in the creation of a Muslim nation for post-independent India.

Appeal for a unified India

Just before the end of the war, Winston Churchill lost the election and the Labour Party came into power. They supported India's call for an independent nation. Muslim League leader Muhammad Ali Jinnah campaigned for a separate Muslim state even as Jawaharlal Nehru asked for a unified India along with Gandhi. There was growing discontent between the Congress Party and the Muslim League—the latter had always strived to get more power for India. India's last British viceroy, Lord Mountbatten, had been given the duty to draw up the roadmap towards Britain's withdrawal from India. Nehru did not want to create two countries out of India and was against the partition, but finally accepted Mountbatten and the Muslim League's plan to divide India.

Lord Mountbatten swears in Pandit Jawaharlal Nehru as the first Prime Minister of free India at the ceremony held at 8.30 am on 15th August, 1947.

1857: First Indian mutiny against the British

1947: India gains freedom

Lord Mountbatten meets Nehru, Jinnah and other leaders to plan the Partition of India.

Earl Mountbatten

WORLD WAR II AND INDIA'S FREEDOM STRUGGLE

India Granted Independence

Overcrowded train transferring refugees during the partition of India, 1947. This was considered to be the largest migration in human history.

In February 1947, Britain announced that India would be granted freedom by June 1948. Indian Viceroy Lord Louis Mountbatten asked for a unified India and requested the Hindus and Muslims to agree to the formation of such a country. Unfortunately, with violence erupting across the country, Mountbatten agreed to form two separate states and changed the date to 15th August, 1947.

Fixing of the border

The partition issue was largely debated and strongly opposed at first. However, once it was clear that the partition would be carried out, the task of fixing a border between the new states assumed grave importance.

Before the partition, the Muslims were living in two main regions in the north that were on the opposite sides of the country. Between these sections remained a huge Hindu population. Moreover, northern India also served as home to several other religions including Sikhs and Christians. To split the nation would also involve splitting the populations of these communities.

While the talks of partition were in progress, the Sikh community also asked for a nation of their own, but their demand was rejected. Finally, it was decided that the border for the two states would be made between Lahore and Amritsar.

The partition

This partition was highly controversial and not without blood; more than 500,000 on both sides lost their lives. Around 10 million people fled from either side to avoid the violence that came with the partition. Thousands of women were abducted during the partition. Cities were swarming with refugees as over 14 million people were crossing borders. Train compartments comprising thousands of refugees were destroyed and passengers were killed.

Pakistan was formed as a new country on 14th August, 1947. On the next day, India was granted its freedom and emerged as an independent country.

On 30th January, 1948, Gandhi was shot by Nathuram Ghodse because of his acceptance to create a multi-religious state.

Nathuram Ghodse

Statue of Gandhi in Bangalore.

HISTORY ENCYCLOPEDIA

Freedom at Midnight

The speech on "Tryst with Destiny" was delivered by Jawaharlal Nehru, independent India's first prime minister in the Indian Constituent Assembly on the eve of India's Independence during midnight on 14th August, 1947. It is considered as one of the greatest speeches as it captured the essence of India's freedom struggle, which, despite certain violent altercations, remained largely peaceful and non-violent against the British Empire in India.

FAST FACT

India awoke to freedom at midnight hour and the Constituent Assembly began its sitting at 11 pm with the singing of Vande Mataram by Sucheta Kripalani.

Excerpts from the speech

Many years ago, we made a tryst with destiny and now the time has come when we shall redeem our pledge, not wholly or in full measure, but very substantially. At the stroke of the midnight hour, when the world sleeps, India will awake to life and freedom. A moment comes, which comes, but rarely in history, when we step out from the old to the new, when an age ends, and when the soul of a nation, long suppressed, finds utterance.

It is fitting that at this solemn moment, we take the pledge of dedication to the service of India and her people, and to the still larger cause of humanity. At the dawn of history India started on her unending quest and trackless centuries, which are filled with her striving and the grandeur of her success and her failures. Through good and ill fortunes alike she has never lost sight of that quest or forgotten the ideals which gave her strength. We end today a period of ill fortunes and India discovers herself again.

The achievement we celebrate today is but a step, an opening of opportunity, to the greater triumphs and achievements that await us. Are we brave enough and wise enough to grasp this opportunity and accept the challenge of the future? Freedom and power bring responsibility. The responsibility rests upon this assembly, a sovereign body representing the sovereign people of India.

Independence Day

At 11:57 pm on the 14th of August, 1947, Pakistan was declared as a separate nation. Even today, this day is celebrated as Independence Day in Pakistan. About five minutes later, at 12:02, India was granted her freedom. It was a memorable moment that came after over an almost 100-year-long struggle for freedom against the British rule. It took many rebellions and the sacrifice of many brave lives, but India was finally a free country.

Jawaharlal Nehru gives his speech.